the world's
BEST
BFFs

the world's
BEST
BFFs

a celebration
of truly perfect
friendships

Written by Nadia Bailey
Illustrations by Juppi Juppsen

**Smith
Street
Books**

AURORA PUBLIC LIBRARY

CONTENTS

WHAT IS A BFF?

Cast your mind back to your childhood years – grade one or the first birthday party you went to where you didn't know anyone. Maybe you sat next to a kid – cool hair, t-shirt of no importance, pen mark on left knee – who turned to you, offered you the red crayon, and from that moment onward you were best friends.

Or maybe you met your best friend at a grade six dance because you liked their sneakers, or maybe you bonded over eye-rolling at dude-bros in your English Lit class or over cheap wine at a house party. Perhaps you met on LiveJournal and drove halfway across the country to meet and got along even better IRL.

Maybe you're the kind of besties that go on adventures together, being smarter, braver, more adventurous than you'd be otherwise. Maybe you challenge each other's ideas or you have a friendly kind of rivalry that helps you push forward in your work and in your life. Maybe you're the type of friends who are happiest doing nothing together – and in those small, quiet moments, when you're reading or watching TV or sitting side by side watching the world go by, you're the most content you'll ever be.

There are many kinds of BFFs featured in these pages – from heroes to stoners, special agents to supermodels. They epitomise the best in humanity's potential to love our fellow humans (and in a couple of cases, our fellow animals). Each pairing has their own particular history and quirks, and each possesses a unique bond that makes their friendship worthy of note.

Study them. Learn from them. Take to heart the lessons that they teach us: that a best friend should be loyal and fierce, accepting and generous, trusting and trustworthy, someone who's there for you when you need them and there for you when you don't even know that you need them.

Perhaps the Spice Girls said it best when they sang, 'If you wanna be my lover, you gotta get with my friends/Make it last forever, friendship never ends.' Lovers may come and go, but a best friend will never leave you. So here's to friendship: glorious, beautiful, messy and inspiring. If you don't have it, never give up until you find it. If you have it, hold on to it. And may it last forever.

ABBI & ILANA

If anyone ever tells you that women aren't funny, sit them down in front of *Broad City* (and also maybe smack them in the face). The show is smart, heartfelt, and shamelessly lowbrow – filled with poop jokes, full-frontal nudity, and on one occasion, a sexual encounter with a tree – and behind it all are Abbi Jacobson and Ilana Glazer, comedy masterminds and real-life BFFs.

These ladies are 100% legit: not only did they create the show but they are also its head writers and stars, and every episode is a lil' love letter to their friendship. It's possible that Abbi and Ilana are the least boring people on television. No, wait – make that on earth.

In real life, their friendship is as solid as they come (they met nearly a decade ago at a weekly practice group at UCB for improv comedians where they were the only two women in the class – they've been best friends ever since). And as characters, they epitomise everything that's worth aspiring to: they're flawed, they're crass, they're hilarious, they're sexy, they're gross and they're always down to clown.

The fictional Abbi and Ilana might be human train wrecks but they're always there for each other: they don't judge each other, or get weird or jealous, or define themselves by whoever they're boning. They're totally clued-up, self-possessed women with a whole lot of swagger. And ultimately, the show's truest romance is their friendship. Can we get a 'YASS, KWEEN'?

Abbi's life motto is, 'When in doubt, make something.' And Ilana's? 'The world is ending. Get pleasure.'

JAY-Z & KANYE

Fun fact: no one really knows for sure if Kanye West and Jay-Z are BFFs or have serious beef.
On one day, Kanye might deliver a very public mid-concert rant about how Hova won't return his calls. On another day they might be spotted in public together or chilling backstage at an awards show like it ain't no thang. They're like the Schrödinger's cat of friendships – unknown, unknowable and in a state of constant flux.

Let's rewind a little. One thing we know for sure is that the two rap gods have worked together since way back when, with Yeezy acting as producer on Jay's 2001 album *The Blueprint*. Over the next decade or so, they worked together, partied together and climbed up that fame ladder together – Kanye infamously defended Beyoncé's honour at the MTV VMAs in 2009, and when they teamed up to record a few tracks for an EP, the creative chemistry was so strong that it turned into a full-length album, *Watch the Throne*.

But it hasn't all been so rosy and there are so many burning questions. Like, why didn't Jay attend Kanye's wedding to Kimmy K? Do their kids really not hang out? Are Kanye's rants for real or is he just doing it to get attention? And could all this supposed drama between them just be a fever dream of the tabloids? Maybe Kanye got it right when he called Jay his big brother, because although brothers might scrap and argue, forget to call or do something dumb that embarrasses the other – and maybe they might even stop speaking for a while – but when it comes down to it, they'll always be there for each other. Because they're family, you know?

At the Grammys I said 'I inspired me' / But my big brother who I always tried to be.

– 'Big Brother', Kanye West

BIG EDIE & LITTLE EDIE

Charming, style-savvy and utterly eccentric, Big Edie and Little Edie are the kind of best friends who need no one but each other. Big Edie (Edith Ewing Bouvier Beale) and her daughter Little Edie (Edith Bouvier Beale) lived together in a crumbling 28-room mansion filled with cats and the spectres of their privileged past – they were relatives of Jacqueline Kennedy Onassis and had once been fixtures of the New York social scene.

When she was young, Big Edie had been a singer, while Little Edie was a famous beauty who'd had a brief career as a model. But over time, they retreated from society to live in a strange world of their own making. The 1975 documentary *Grey Gardens*, directed by Albert and David Maysles, allowed an intimate and moving glimpse into the Beales' world, in which everything was a performance: Big Edie sings hits from the 1940s like an opera star, while Little Edie marches and dances like a majorette. They bicker constantly, sit in bed and eat ice-cream with one another, and drink wine from Dixie cups. They believe in ghosts and don't have running water. There are cats everywhere, and they staunchly co-habitate with wild raccoons, possums and fleas. At the same time, they are always glamorous, always turned out: they get around the house in swimsuits worn with high heels, a turban fashioned from a sweater fixed with a sparkling brooch, or a skirt worn upside down with fishnet stockings and a cape.

Their friendship is heartwarming and tragic and poignant all at the same time. Part Miss Havisham, part *Sunset Boulevard*, they inhabited a world of equal parts squalor and glamour. But no matter what: they had each other.

Little Edie signed off letters to her mother with, 'With ladles and ladles of kisses, loves & hugs – your ever precious, ever loving and ever darling and kissable Edes.'

AMY & TINA

With more than two glorious decades of friendship behind them, Tina Fey and Amy Poehler are the living embodiment of friendship goals. Separately, they are smart, formidable, endearing, and knee-bucklingly funny. Together, they are a force of comedy to be reckoned with, a duo whose shtick has only gotten better, brighter and funnier over the years.

These legends have brought us the absolute cream of *SNL* (see: the Mom Jeans sketch or the time Amy was Hillary Clinton to Tina's Sarah Palin), given us the only good reason to watch the *Golden Globes,* and made *Mean Girls*, aka the most quotable movie of all time ('She doesn't even go here!'). Oh, and separately we can thank Tina for giving us Liz Lemon, and Amy for Leslie Knope, as well as being involved in a host of other shows and movies that have made your life worth living. What did we do to deserve such benevolence?

We can also thank these two for taking on the comedy scene boy's club and totally killing it. While it seems kind of naff to point out that they're – shock! – female comedians, without their successes paving the way, we might never have gotten to see other kick-ass comics like Kristen Wiig, Kate McKinnon, Amy Schumer or the *Broad City* gals doing their thing either.

From the moment they met in an improv class in 1993 all the way through hosting the *Golden Globes* together, their friendship has served as a beacon of goodness. It reminds us that friends should be kind and supportive and take joy in photobombing each other. They're not just two of the greatest comedians of our time, they're also two of the greatest humans. Tina, Amy: thank you for all you've given us.

'I think that Tina and I are chosen sisters. I think we are chosen family.'

– Amy Poehler

15

SIR IAN &
SIR PATRICK

Sir Patrick Stewart is a man of many talents. To Trekkies, he's Captain of the Starship Enterprise. To the comic book crowd, he's Professor Charles Xavier. To theatre lovers, he's one of the most renowned Shakespearean actors of his generation. But to Sir Ian McKellen, he'll always be one thing: his best friend.

These living legends have a lot in common: they're both old-school thespians who built lauded careers as serious theatre players, and then made the leap into mainstream film and television (Sir Patrick with his role as Captain Jean-Luc Picard in *Star Trek: The Next Generation* and Sir Ian as the title character in the film adaptation of Shakespeare's *Richard III*). They're both around the same age, both staunch in their political activism, and both have been knighted for services to drama and the performing arts. And yes, they regularly refer to each other as 'Sir Ian' and 'Sir Patrick'.

While they first met in England in the theatre scene, it wasn't until they were both cast in Bryan Singer's blockbuster *X-Men* that they really hit it off. From there, their friendship blossomed into something truly beautiful – spanning five *X-Men* films, two theatrical collaborations and about a million memes. The Sirs regularly show up to support each other's red carpet events, hang out in their downtime and even cook for each other. And the best bit? Sir Ian became an ordained minister of the Universal Life Church in 2013 so that he could preside on Sir Patrick's wedding day. This truly is a bromance for the ages.

When asked to create a hashtag that described their friendship, Sir Patrick chose #arentwelucky and Sir Ian chose #eternal.

MATT & BEN

From childhood besties who bonded over Dungeons & Dragons to two of the most bankable film stars in the world, Matt Damon and Ben Affleck sure have come a long way together.

From humble beginnings growing up two blocks from each other in Cambridge, Massachusetts, it's always been clear that they're two of a kind: both knew from an early age they wanted to be actors, both got fed up waiting to be cast in a film that would launch their careers, and both decided to take matters into their own hands.

In a genius move, Matt and Ben decided to write their own movie – and also cast themselves in the lead roles. What's a bestie for if they can't write you a juicy part in an Oscar-winning movie, right? The film was 1997's *Good Will Hunting*, which was directed by Gus Van Sant, co-starred Robin Williams and Ben's kid brother, Casey, and cemented the two Boston boys as major new talents.

Since then, their careers have gone from strength to strength – as actors, they've worked with almost every legendary director, from Martin Scorsese to Steven Soderbergh and David Fincher. They've achieved both critical and popular acclaim, founded two production companies, and firmly established themselves in the Hollywood big-time (Matt with the *Bourne Identity* franchise and Ben as Batman in the latest incarnation of the DC Universe).

And sure, there have been times when their careers have gone a little off track or they've been on the wrong end of tabloid gossip, but they've never let that impact their solid gold love for each other. Even cuter? Now that they've both been married and had families, their kids are all pals too. The Damon–Affleck love-fest continues.

'If you put us together, you might actually make a whole, creative, interesting individual.'
– Matt Damon

OPRAH & GAYLE

Oprah Winfrey and Gayle King first met as co-workers just starting out in the media biz. Oprah was a news anchor and Gayle was a production assistant for the same Baltimore news station.

One snowy night, the future most-famous-talk-show-host-ever invited Gayle to stay at her place so she wouldn't have to brave the terrible weather. They stayed up all night and discovered they had a lot in common: both grew up in predominantly white neighbourhoods, both loved Barry Manilow and Neil Diamond, both were in their early 20s, and both were single. By morning, a glorious friendship had formed.

The two have been inseparable ever since – when Oprah launched her magazine, she asked Gayle to quit her job as a TV anchor so they could work on it together; Gayle had her own show on Oprah's network; Oprah was maid-of-honour at Gayle's wedding; and they love going on vacation together. In fact, they are so close that they've been fending off rumours that they're more than just friends for years.

Oprah told *O* magazine in 2006, 'I understand why people think we're gay. There isn't a definition in our culture for this kind of bond between women. So I get why people have to label it – how can you be this close without it being sexual? How else can you explain a level of intimacy where someone always loves you, always respects you, admires you?'

Their love is strong, deep, and sincere. This is a friendship that has withstood time, distance, a touch of professional rivalry and one half of the duo being one of the most famous people in the world. Has it changed their friendship? Not a bit (well, except for the fact that now Oprah has a 'Gayle wing' in her house). They still call each other about four times a day – just like they did back in Baltimore.

'There is not a better human being in the world as far as I'm concerned.'

– Oprah Winfrey

Lots of people want to ride with you in the limo ...

but what you want is someone who will take the bus with you when the limo breaks down.

– Oprah Winfrey

CARRIE & GARY

Carrie Fisher's friendship with Gary began in New York at what Carrie described as, 'a very tragic pet store'. She wasn't meant to be buying a pet. But there he was, one of those poor puppy-mill dogs who's just a little bit NQR – bulging eyes, nuggety body, and a too-long tongue that hung out the side of his mouth like he was a cartoon character. It was, as they say, love at first sight.

Forming the kind of close attachment that would rival Han and Chewbacca's, Carrie and Gary became inseparable: he'd accompany her on the red carpet, sit by her side during interviews and book signings, and travel across the country with her. A lesser dog might have been eclipsed by Carrie's larger-than-life personality and superstar status, but not Gary. Gary became a star in his own right, thanks to his complete nonchalance and DGAF attitude (this is the kind of dog who straight up falls asleep in front of a crowd of snapping paparazzi and once tried to fight BB-8 during a press appearance in London).

Gary was so important to Carrie that she had him registered as a therapy dog so that he could legally accompany her everywhere. Always open about her mental health and struggles with drug abuse and bipolar disorder, Carrie relied on Gary's company for the kind of emotional support and unconditional love that is at the heart of any great friendship. Gary was by Carrie's side when she went into cardiac arrest aboard a flight from London to Los Angeles in December, 2016. He remained with her at the hospital until she died four days later, proving that he was the truest and best of friends.

'Gary is like my heart. Gary is very devoted to me, and that calms me down. He's anxious when he's away from me.'

– Carrie Fisher

MARILYN & ELLA

Legend has it, when Marilyn Monroe was studying to be a singer, her coach told her to track down a particular recording of a little-known jazz vocalist and listen to the album a hundred times. She did, and she developed a profound appreciation for the musician's skill, soul and artistry. The singer's name was Ella Fitzgerald.

Later down the line, the two singers had the opportunity to meet as they often played the same small jazz clubs. By this point, Marilyn was already well on her way to becoming a superstar – but she made a point to befriend Ella, whose voice and style had had such an impact on her own performance. The two had a lot in common: both came from poor backgrounds, both were self-made women, and both loved the sultry, glamorous nightlife of the jazz scene.

The most important venue in Hollywood at the time was the Mocambo, a Latin-themed club on Sunset Strip, where the walls were lined with glass cages full of live cockatoos, macaws and parrots (in other words, it was the definition of extra). On any night, you could find the hottest jazz singers on stage, and in the audience, a heady mix of Hollywood royalty, from Marlene Dietrich to Clark Gable.

Although Ella was already forging a brilliant career, the Mocambo's owners refused to book her – by some accounts it was because she was not well known, but most make it clear that it was because she was African-American. Marilyn called up the club's owner and made him an offer he couldn't refuse: if he booked Ella, she would reserve a front-row table every night she performed. Years later, Ella would recall, 'Marilyn was there, front table, every night. The press went overboard. After that, I never had to play a small jazz club again.'

'She was an unusual woman – a little ahead of her time. And she didn't know it.'

– Ella Fitzgerald

ANN & LESLIE

Find yourself a best friend who knows how to give you a compliment that's straight from the heart. You'll know it when you hear it, because it will be beautiful. It will be creative. It will be unique to you. For inspiration, look no further than Leslie Knope of *Parks and Recreation,* and her ability to pay the best kind of compliments to her best friend, Ann Perkins. Like, for example: 'Oh, Ann, you beautiful, rule-breaking moth,' and 'Ann, you poetic noble land mermaid.'

Ann and Leslie's friendship is built on love, trust, honesty, mutual respect and a willingness to get completely wastey-face with each other. To Leslie, Ann is an 'opalescent tree shark'. Ann supports Leslie and keeps her grounded no matter what hijinks she gets herself into – but she also isn't afraid to give Leslie the hard truths about her relationships or ability to wear tulip skirts. Leslie always prioritises Ann's happiness, including giving her permission to date a guy she used to have a thing for, because she believes absolutely putting her friends first: 'You know my code, hoes before bros. Uteruses before duderuses. Ovaries before brovaries.'

And as a lasting gift to BFFs of the female persuasion everywhere, it was Leslie who invented the beautiful tradition of Galentine's Day (it's only the best day of the year!) – a day to celebrate all the amazing women in your life and remember that dudes may come and go, but it's the beautiful, glowing, sun goddesses in your life who'll always be there. Just like Ann and Leslie are for each other.

'Ann, you beautiful tropical fish. You're smart as a whip and you're cool under pressure.'

– Leslie Knope

Ann, you are such a good friend ...

You're a beautiful, talented, brilliant, powerful musk-ox.

– Leslie Knope

ALEXANDER & ISABELLA

Some people are so rare that they are just not meant for this world. So it was with Alexander McQueen and Isabella Blow, two brilliant misfits who found and lost each other in one of history's most tragic tales of friendship.

The pair met in the early 90s, when Alexander – then known by his birth name, Lee – presented his graduate collection at the prestigious fashion school Central Saint Martins. Isabella was so taken with it that she decided to buy the whole collection on the spot (a move typical of the woman with a reputation for wild outfits, wilder business decisions and an enduring love of hats).

Isabella convinced Lee to go by his middle name, Alexander (because it sounded more regal) and a fashion label – and friendship – was born. Proving herself worthy of BFF status, she moved Alexander into her flat, introduced him to the right people, and helped secure his place in the London elite's social circles.

Alexander and Issie's bond ran deep – both were fiercely creative and wildly insecure. She was his muse and benefactor, and he was a frequent houseguest at the country estate she owned with her husband Detmar. Alexander frequently drew on Isabella's ideas, and on one occasion, invited her to walk in his runway show.

But as with many friendships between larger-than-life personalities, things didn't always run smoothly: the pair had a falling out when Issie introduced the McQueen label to Tom Ford but received no recognition or payment when the Gucci Group acquired a majority share in Alexander's company. But despite a few volatile times, the pair remained close for over 15 years, until, tragically, Isabella died by suicide in 2007.

According to friends, Alexander asked a medium to get in contact with Isabella after her death. He was told, 'Isabella is with her grandmother. She is happy, and wishes everyone would not be so sad.'

RUPAUL & MICHELLE

You! Better! Work! Because these best friends are as fabulous as they come. In one corner, the genre-defining supermodel of the world who stands six-feet-four-inches before heels and hairdo, the spirit animal for gays, queens and the identity-fluid. In the other corner, *Drag Race*'s resident den mother, a woman of quick wit, strong opinions and gigantic hair. Strike your best pose for RuPaul and Michelle Visage!

Together, these two make up the heart and soul of *RuPaul's Drag Race*. They are strong. They are kind. They are the definition of extra. And they have mad love for each other: when RuPaul landed a radio spot on WKTU back in the early 90s,

Michelle was his co-host. Ru brought her on for *The RuPaul Show* on VH1, then onwards and upwards to *RuPaul's Drag Race*. Together they create television magic, delivering episode after episode of shade-throwing, lip-synching and utter drag queen realness.

With a quarter of a century of friendship behind them, they always knew they were destined to be friends. Michelle told *Spin* in 2013 that in the early days of their acquaintance, she ran into Ru at an event and wasn't sure if he would remember her. But she needn't have worried. 'Bitch, stop right there,' Ru said. 'Not only do I remember you, I used to watch you at the Red Zone seeing you perform, and I go that bitch is a *star*. Your little blonde ass boppin' all around. I had my eye on you for years.' Amen to that, sister.

'I can look at him and know what he's thinking. I don't even get that with my husband. It's a crazy, soulmate scenario in a gay man/hetero woman sort of way.'

– Michelle Visage

DAVID & IGGY

Imagine it: the year is 1976 and David Bowie has asked Iggy Pop to tag along on his *Station to Station* tour. They already know each other, of course – they first met in '71, and Iggy's wild stage presence was a partial inspiration for David's Ziggy Stardust persona – but this is the first time they've really spent time on the road together. Both are coming out of a period of drug abuse and creative transition, with Iggy having split from the Stooges and David reaching the end of his Ziggy phase and transforming into the Thin White Duke.

On the road, they develop a cosy, almost domestic routine – listening to music on the long drives between shows, or talking late into the night. Sometimes, they just sit there, sipping espressos and reading, without feeling obliged to chat, like an old married couple. Their friendship deepens. So much so, in fact, that they decide to move to West Berlin together where they share an apartment. It's there that their creative partnership blossoms: David begins working on the first album in what would become known as his Berlin trilogy, and they collaborate on writing and recording Iggy's first solo album, *The Idiot*, and later his seminal album, *Lust for Life*.

Years later, following Bowie's death, Iggy would tell *The New York Times* that David had saved him. 'The friendship was basically that this guy salvaged me from certain professional and maybe personal annihilation – simple as that. A lot of people were curious about me, but only he was the one who had enough truly in common with me, and who actually really liked what I did and could get on board with it, and who also had decent enough intentions to help me out. He did a good thing.'

'David's friendship was the light of my life. I never met such a brilliant person. He was the best there is.'

– Iggy Pop

KIRK & SPOCK

They're *Star Trek*'s classic odd couple: Captain James T. Kirk, the hot-headed adventurer to whom the words 'dashing', 'impulsive', and 'damn, what a player' would apply. And Spock, the coolly rational scientist who never lets his emotions sway his impeccably reasoned logic.

At first they clashed – Spock believes Kirk's tendency to make decisions based on gut instinct is dangerous; Kirk thinks Spock is little better than a robot – but over time, they developed a productive working relationship and an abiding respect for each other's point of view. While Kirk is driven by passion, he comes to rely on Spock's level-headed advice, especially when it comes to sharing the burdens of command. But even more significantly, he values Spock's opinion even beyond the borders of their professional relationship – he looks to Spock's insight in all things, because he knows it would never stem from a place of self-interest or be swayed by petty emotional concerns.

Their friendship blooms slowly, across years and galaxies, as they explore strange new worlds, seek out new civilisations, and boldly go where no besties have gone before. And since Spock would never be the kind of guy to be effusive in his affection, the few times he does admit to his devotion to Kirk are made all the more meaningful. We dare you to watch Spock sacrifice himself for Kirk, professing, 'I have been – and always shall be – your friend,' and not cry approximately one million tears.

This is a friendship that neither time nor death can touch, between a man of action and an unemotional, yet fiercely loyal, alien who could express more happiness, sorrow, or pain with a quirk of one eyebrow than most of us could express with words. May their love live long and prosper.

'Of my friend, I can only say this: of all the souls I have encountered in my travels, his was the most ... human.'

– Captain James Kirk

HACHIKŌ & PROF UENO

In 1924, Hidesaburō Ueno, an agriculture professor at the University of Tokyo, adopted a golden brown Akita Inu. He named the dog Hachikō, *hachi* meaning 'eight' and *kō* meaning 'affection'. Every day, Ueno would commute to work by train, and at the end of each day, Hachikō would be waiting at Shibuya Station for his best friend to return so that the two of them could walk home together.

One day, Professor Ueno set off as usual, and, as usual, at the end of the day Hachikō trotted to the station to meet him. But Professor Ueno did not return that day. Tragically, he had suffered a cerebral haemorrhage while giving a lecture, and died without ever returning to the train station where Hachikō was patiently waiting.

There was no way for the dog to know what had happened to his master, so every evening, Hachikō would go to the station to wait for Ueno to return. At first, no one knew why he waited at the station every day, until one of Professor Ueno's students happened to recognise Hachikō and followed him to the home of the professor's former gardener. The student returned frequently to visit Hachikō, and went on to write several articles about the dog's incredible loyalty, which elevated Hachikō to something of a national hero.

For the next nine years, nine months and 15 days, Hachikō waited for his master in vain. Hachikō passed away on 8 March, 1935 – a dog who truly earned the title of 'man's best friend'. After his death, Hachikō was cremated and his ashes were buried in Aoyama Cemetery, Tokyo, where they rest beside those of his beloved master. What did we do to deserve dogs?

Nippon Cultural Broadcasting in Japan managed to recover a recording of Hachikō from an old record that had been broken into pieces. On Saturday, 28 May, 1994 – 59 years after his death – millions of people tuned in to hear Hachikō barking once more.

FRODO & SAM

If your best friend was possessed by dark enchantments forged in the fire of Mount Doom that slowly sucked all the goodness and light out of him and left him an empty shell instead of the sunny boy from the Shire you grew up with, would you stand by him? Well, Samwise Gamgee would.

From JRR Tolkien's *The Lord of the Rings*, Sam is a Hobbit with a heart of gold. His love, devotion and loyalty to Frodo Baggins never wavers. As the two of them deal with Orcs and Dark Riders, giant spiders and evil wizards, as war rages around them and empires crumble, the two Hobbits are steadfast in their friendship – Frodo increasingly corrupted by the power of the One Ring, and Sam determined to keep the dark forces at bay. In fact, it's this very

goodness and kindness that overcomes the terrible power of the Ring. 'Come on, Mr Frodo,' says Sam, when they finally make it to Mount Doom. 'I can't carry it for you ... but I can carry you.' THIS GUY.

Frodo might be the hero of the story, but Sam is its heart: he's the kind of friend who'll drop everything to accompany his bestie on a quest that will almost certainly end in death, and the guy who will stand by his BFF no matter how ensorcelled by ancient, terrible magic he is, *and* do it all with a smile. It is entirely possible that Frodo doesn't deserve such goodness. The lesson here? Get yourself a friend who'll stick with you through the tough times as well as the good – cos you never know when a wizard might call you to go on a quest and you'll need a friend who not only has your back, but also always remembers to pack something to eat for elevenses.

'*I am glad you are here with me. Here at the end of all things, Sam.*'
– *Frodo Baggins*

KATE & NAOMI

Shout out to everyone who's ever spent a late night Googling 'Kate Moss Naomi Campbell 90s' and then felt mildly depressed that you can never hope to be as cool as these two icons. We feel you.

Kate and Naomi are the OG supermodel queens: they first met on a fashion shoot in 1992. Naomi thought that Kate was strikingly beautiful and knew right away that there was something special about the shy young model. They crossed paths again some months later in Madrid, and since Kate didn't know anyone, Naomi decided to take her under her wing. Proving that the modelling industry isn't the bitchy scene it's made out to be, Kate and Naomi, along with fellow model Christy Turlington, became each other's family. 'We were like sisters,' Naomi says. 'Kate and I were a backbone of support for each other.'

To look at photos of them during this time is to receive a lesson in cool: there they are posing with Super Soakers in some dreamy tropical location, getting rowdy in the front row at fashion week and looking the glammest ever in slinky silver Versace. The kind of girls to work hard and play hard, these two were never far apart during the supermodel era, and their friendship continues today. And while both models are notoriously cagey about their private lives, their love for each other is one thing they're more than happy to sound off on. For Kate's 40th birthday, Naomi penned an open letter in the *Evening Standard* about her BFF which laid bare just how much they mean to each other. 'Kate and I have seen each other through the good and the bad. Kate has stood by me through it all. You can count on your hands the friends who'll be there for you in the tough times, and she's one of them.'

'We're like we're at secondary school. That's what happens with girlfriends who've grown up together. That's the charm of the friendship.'

– Naomi Campbell

Friendship is the hardest thing in the world to explain. It's not something you learn in school.

But if you haven't learned the meaning of friendship, you really haven't learned anything.

– Muhammad Ali

MULDER & SCULLY

A word of advice from Fox Mulder: trust no one. Well, almost no one. There's one exception to the rule, and that's Dana Scully – special agent, scientist, sceptic, and the best friend that any alien hunter could hope for.

Although Scully was originally sent to spy on Mulder and report on what the FBI's most misfit child was up to, they formed a bond that went way beyond a working relationship and deep into BFF territory. Theirs is the kind of friendship that's based on challenging each other's ideas: he fervently believes in aliens, sprawling government conspiracies and goat demons called El Chupacabra. She's a scientist who needs tangible evidence before she'll draw any kind of conclusion. Where he sees vampires, she sees a rare genetic condition. Where she sees mass hysteria, he sees proof of demonic possession. But over the course of their friendship, Mulder opens Scully's mind to things that exist beyond the realms of rational comprehension. And she teaches him that no matter how much you want there to be a convoluted government plot undermining your every move, sometimes it's the simplest explanation that's the correct one.

And do they love each other? Heck yes, they do. You can see it in Scully's unwavering loyalty to Mulder, even when her own job, reputation – or life – is at stake. And you can see it in that time Mulder told Scully she was his one in five billion. While fierce debate has raged throughout *The X-Files*' run as to whether the heart of their relationship is platonic or romantic (show creator Chris Carter claims the former, while most fans would ardently disagree), the undeniable truth is that their bond is deeper and more complex to fit either of those labels, and no matter how many shadowy government figures try to rip them apart, their friendship remains as bright as a pair of mysterious lights in the sky and as long lasting as rumours of an alien crash site at Roswell.

'You were my friend and you told me the truth... Even when the world was falling apart, you were my constant. My touchstone.'
— Fox Mulder

BUFFY & WILLOW

How do you survive living on the Hellmouth? You keep your wits and your friends about you.

Buffy Summers is the Chosen One – a teenage vampire slayer tasked with keeping the forces of darkness at bay and the world's final defence against demons, werewolves and government experiments gone horribly awry. The life of a Slayer is a lonely one, but Buffy bucks the trend when she meets Willow Rosenberg – a sweet, socially awkward nerd – who, along with Xander, Cordelia and a rag-tag bunch of misfits, form the Scooby gang. But it's Buffy and Willow's relationship that forms the heart of the group: they're just a couple of teenage girls trying to get through high school, while also contending with Buffy's responsibilities as a Slayer, Willow's burgeoning talent as a witch, and the ongoing threat of living in the most vampire-infested suburb in the world.

Between fighting demons and fending off the apocalypse for about the hundredth time, they still find time for the important things: like giving each other relationship advice, having study dates and sleepovers, and being supportive through each other's toughest moments (say, when Buffy's boyfriend Angel lost his soul and went on a murderous rampage, or when they had to sit their finals). And although Buffy likes to see herself as the lone warrior type, and the only thing standing between the world and utter demonic chaos, through Willow she learns how to rely on her friends – and is stronger for it. She may be the Chosen One, but when it comes to friendship, it's the one she chose that makes her into a real hero.

'There's only one thing on this earth more powerful than evil, and that's us.'
– Buffy Summers

TROY & ABED

Troy Barnes and Abed Nadir of *Community* **are friends so close that they once graced the cover of** *Friends Weekly* – a magazine they made up in order to celebrate their own friendship.

They're a duo united by their abiding love of pop culture, their overactive imaginations and deeply profound weirdness, and they are living proof that no matter how niche your interests are, there is someone out there who has the same appreciation for trying to execute the perfect Batman voice that you do.

They are the kind of friends who have a secret handshake, and create and host their own talk show called *Troy and Abed in the Morning!* These BFFs would follow the other across space, time and into the depths of their most surreal fantasies (like that time Troy almost believed that Abed had become a cartoon and was ready to follow him into a 2D world by running at a brick wall). Together, they give each other permission to be the sweet, loving, obsessive, nerdy oddballs that they are.

In fact, the only time their friendship was ever under threat was when they took an attempt to make the world's largest blanket fort a little too seriously and went to war over two rival countries of their own creations, The United Forts of Pillowtown and The Legit Republic of Blanketsburg. The twenty short minutes of war between these best friends is truly upsetting to see – topped only by the time that Troy decided to leave Greendale to go on a solo adventure with LeVar Burton. It was heartbreaking, but ultimately necessary: parting is an inevitable fact of life, and sometimes the greatest thing we can do for our friends is to encourage them to follow their dreams.

'Abed is a magical elf-like man who makes us all more magical by being near him.'

– Troy Barnes

BARACK & JOE

It's not often we get giddy over politicians, but in the case of former US President Barack Obama and his VP Joe Biden, the fandom is 100% real (and all the more poignant given that their time in office is over). After trying and failing to run for Prez himself a couple of times, Joe joined Barack's ticket for the 2008 election. Barack made the announcement via a text message that read, 'I've chosen Joe Biden to be my running mate.'

At first, people thought it was a weird match – Barry O being the cerebral type who doesn't do drama, and Joe being more of a heart-and-soul kinda guy. So it was a surprise to everyone when Joe became so much more than a running mate, and the two of them became the BFFs that America – no, the world – needed, inspiring the cutest, most heartwarming memes since the internet discovered cats.

Over their eight years in office together, we watched their relationship evolve from the usual handshakes and back-slapping of political allies, to a full on bromance that runs as deep as they come. They weren't just making important political decisions together; they were having weekly lunch dates, cracking each other up, going out for ice-cream and playing golf together in their downtime. Their friendship, played out in the most public of arenas, is entirely genuine. In fact, Barack went so far as to award his bestie the Presidential Medal of Freedom. Nawwww.

And as if all that wasn't enough, they went all fourth grade on us and made matching friendship bracelets (Barack's has a flower charm and a star charm, and Joe's has a smiley face and a slice of pie. We're not crying, YOU'RE crying!). In his final presidential address, Barack acknowledged Joe and his wife, saying, 'We love you and Jill like family and your friendship has been one of the great joys of our life.' Oh boy, it's getting dusty in here.

'A brother to me, a best friend forever.'
– Joe Biden

WILBUR & CHARLOTTE

As far as friends go, you'd be hard pressed to do better than Charlotte. A spider of unparalleled kindness, wisdom and spelling smarts, Charlotte is the kind of friend who would do *anything* to help her pals. *Charlotte's Web* is a story about life, death and a profoundly caring friendship between the titular Charlotte and Wilbur, the unwanted runt of a litter of piglets.

After being sent to a lonely barn, Wilbur tries to befriend some of the animals on the farm, but to no avail. Wilbur is alone and friendless until one night he hears a voice in the darkness that says, 'Do you want a friend, Wilbur? I'll be a friend to you.' That voice belongs to Charlotte, and the two strike up a truly special friendship.

Their mutual appreciation is a joy: Charlotte recognises Wilbur's kindness and eagerness to please. Wilbur is delighted by Charlotte's skill and beauty. So when Wilbur finds out that he's being fattened up for slaughter, his friend springs into action to literally save his bacon. Charlotte starts a one-spider campaign to let the world know of all Wilbur's finest qualities, spinning the words 'some pig', 'terrific', 'radiant' and 'humble' into her webs. Through her words, people begin to see Wilbur for who he is and Wilbur becomes even more of a terrific, radiant, humble pig due to her presence in his life. And though Charlotte ultimately sacrifices herself to save her best friend, she leaves behind the most important of legacies: the lesson that it's through the eyes and hearts of our friends that we become our best selves, and that each of us has the potential to be radiant and terrific, too.

'Wilbur never forgot Charlotte. Although he loved her children and grandchildren dearly, none of the new spiders ever quite took her place in his heart. She was in a class by herself. It is not often that someone comes along who is a true friend and a good writer. Charlotte was both.'

– E.B. White, **Charlotte's Web**

BEYONCÉ & SOLANGE

Solange and Beyoncé Knowles are BFFs of the most inspirational kind. Beyoncé is a woman of grace, class and inner steel who's built a career – no, an empire – that will go down in history as one of pop music's greatest. Solange is no less iconic: she's the arty, underground type who's more interested in flexing her creativity than being a commercial success.

And sure, they're sisters, but their bond goes beyond just sharing the same blood – they're 100% on each other's team, in music, in life, and in elevators.

While Bey's career has been popping off since her Destiny's Child days, the pair made history in 2016 when they each released a No. 1 album as solo artists with *Lemonade* and *A Seat at the Table*. In case you're wondering, that's never happened before (nope, not even the Minogue sisters managed to pull off that trick). Both albums are smart, complex and highly political, with both sisters expressing their lived experience: of being a woman, of being a creator, of being black, of living through this particular moment in history.

And while Solange has always been the cool girl flying under the radar, her latest release has placed her squarely in the spotlight. Bey once sang, 'My sister told me I should speak my mind,' and she's taken that lesson to heart, evolving from pop queen to an unapologetic voice for black activism. They've influenced each other in the most profound of ways – always supportive, always protective, always putting each other first. Solange said it best when she described Bey as, 'the most patient, loving, wonderful sister ever.' Yeah, these two are pretty ***Flawless.

'Solange is the one person I will fight for. Don't talk about my sister; don't play with me about my sister. If you do, you'll see another side of me.'

– Beyoncé Knowles

SELENA & TAYLOR

By the size of her squad, you'd be forgiven for thinking that Taylor Swift is all about quantity over quality. But there's one girl who is first among equals, who's been there from the beginning, and holds a special place in Tay's heart (and Instagram). That girl is Selena Gomez.

The pair became besties back in 2008 when they were both dating Jonas Brothers (Taylor was dating Joe and Selena was dating Nick), and they instantly hit it off. And while their relationships with the Jonases may have ended, their friendship went from strength to strength – and no break-up, world tour or dalliance with Justin Bieber could ever get in their way.

And even though they're two of the biggest stars in the world, the two pop baes have a refreshingly normal friendship: they are two founding members of the Lonely Girls Club, an essential girl-time activity that involved going over to Taylor's house to chill out, scarf down junk food, and bond over the fact that they were single. And if you haven't done that with your bestie, quite frankly, you haven't lived.

As with most high-profile friendships, there's always going to be speculation that they're secretly feuding or that one of them hates the other's new boyfriend. But though the tabloids love to stoke the rumours that these two besties have beef, in actuality they're all good, thanks. They're strong and true and they'll defend each other to the end. After all, it's not just anyone who Tay calls 'the closest thing I've ever had to a sister'. And no matter how many people Tay brings into her circle, Selena will always be No. 1 in her squad.

'Every single problem I ever have is healable by Taylor Swift.'

– Selena Gomez

FEDERICO & SALVADOR

No one really knows for sure if Salvador Dalí and Federico García Lorca were friends or lovers, but what is clear is that they had the kind of electric connection that challenged and inspired them to become better artists and more complete people. The painter and the poet have gone down in history as one of the most fiercely creative duos the world has ever seen.

Salvador and Federico first crossed paths in Madrid in 1923 when they were both students living at the Residencia de Estudiantes – it all began when Federico spotted Salvador and was captivated by his outlandish sense of style, while Salvador was drawn to Federico's poetic spirit, and the fact that he knew everyone worth knowing. While they had wildly different temperaments – Salvador was self-conscious and shy, while Federico was vivacious and made friends everywhere – they quickly formed an attachment.

Theirs was a friendship built on not only supporting but challenging each other. They frequently disagreed about art and literature – Federico liked to draw on tradition and folklore in his poetry and plays, while Salvador was all about modernity and pushing the boundaries of taste, style and art itself. They developed a deep bond which is documented in a series of passionate letters: 'You are a Christian storm and you are in need of some of my paganism,' wrote Salvador in a typically cryptic note. 'I will go get you and give you some seaside medicine. It will be winter and we will light a fire. The poor beasts will be trembling with the cold. You will recall that you are an inventor of marvellous things and we will live together with a portrait machine ...' Federico returned the favour by writing an epic eight-page poem called 'Ode to Salvador Dali.'

The two were so close that they developed their own private language of motifs and images in their letters to each other. Federico described their bond as being like 'twin spirits'.

PATTI & ROBERT

Robert Mapplethorpe and Patti Smith were two halves of a whole. When they met quite by chance in New York City, they were both poor, creative and trying to eke out a living – in each other, they recognised kindred spirits.

Sometime lovers but all-time friends, these two artists were united by the belief that there's no excuse for a life lived dully or ungenerously. Together, they brought the world a little more magic: for Robert, it was via his beautiful but confronting photographs that foregrounded homosexual eroticism, and for Patti, through her poetry, her art and her music. No matter where they were, they looked for beauty in the world.

Which brings us to the duo's inherent sense of wonder – a trait they embodied their whole lives, before Robert was cruelly taken too soon. This was a pair known to make powerful talismans out of the most banal of objects, wear incredible vintage clothing, find joy in sharing a Coney Island hotdog and take spiritual nourishment from art (even when there was no money to buy food). They abhorred notions of conventionality, compromise and commercial appeal.

What they had been searching for, says Patti, was, 'a lover and a friend to create with, side by side. To be loyal, yet to be free.' When they found each other, they woke up knowing that they were no longer alone. In art and in life, they were true soulmates. They were each other's everything.

'I thought to myself that he contained a whole universe that I had yet to know.'

– Patti Smith

world's best BFFs

JRR & CS

Two giants of the fantasy genre, Clive Staples Lewis and John Ronald Reuel Tolkien first met in 1926 in the hallowed halls of Oxford University. At their first meeting, Lewis described Tolkien as a 'smooth, pale, fluent little chap' – and although that first impression wasn't necessarily the most flattering, they soon discovered they had a lot in common.

Both great men of letters had fought in World War I. Both studied and taught classical subjects like the literatures of medieval romance and Norse mythology. And both loved storytelling. They tinkered away on their respective projects at an informal literary discussion group at Oxford called The Inklings, where they were each other's first and most supportive audience while building the foundations for brand new worlds like Narnia and Middle Earth.

Another thing they bonded over? A shared hatred of Walt Disney. The two once went on a movie date to see *Snow White and the Seven Dwarfs* – and both hated it. Specifically, they were horrified by the depiction of the dwarfs – Lewis by their 'bloated, drunken, low comedy faces' and Tolkien by the fact that the dwarves in his own work were a grim and powerful people, rather than a bunch of jolly, goofy miners. Whether they were united by hating on a popular film or getting deep with each other about the existence of God (Tolkien is credited for reigniting Lewis's Christian faith), these two fantasy bigwigs were always there for each other.

It's true that the two had their differences over the years – there was definitely an element of professional rivalry at play as well as theological rifts – but when CS died, JRR felt the loss deeply. In a letter to his daughter, he wrote that he felt 'like an old tree that is losing all its leaves one by one: this feels like an axe-blow near the roots'.

Tolkien based Treebeard's mannerisms on Lewis's, giving the leader of the Ents his friend's booming voice and habit of constant throat-clearing.

MARY-KATE & ASHLEY

Every now and then, the world delivers a pair of best friends so cool, so aspirational and so damn perfect that all we can do is bow down and cry out that we're not worthy. And none more so than Mary-Kate and Ashley Olsen, once child stars, now fashion designers and forever the ultimate in friendship goals.

The twins have been famous ever since they crawled into the public eye sharing the role of *Full House*'s Michelle Tanner at nine months old, and over the years, we've grown up with them: from their adorable baby TV actor stage and their cute-as-a-button straight-to-video movie stage, to their transformation into street style icons in the late 00s, and then onwards and upwards to becoming legit players in the fashion biz. Ashley is older by two and

a half minutes and is an inch taller. Mary-Kate is the quieter, more reflective one. They speak on the phone multiple times a day, and always end the call by saying, 'Love you.' Throughout their very long, very public career, one thing has remained the same: their utter devotion to each other.

You could be forgiven for thinking that they're basically two halves of a single entity. But according to Mary-Kate, they're actually very different. 'I think that's why we work so well together – it's the yin and the yang,' she says. 'When she's up, I'm down and when I'm down, she's up. We're always sort of balancing each other out and encouraging each other ... It's like talking about friends. You're different than your best friend; you're two completely different people.' But like the yin and yang, you can't have one without the other and it's only together that they're truly complete.

'We're very close, we're extremely close. I completely understand her and she completely understands me.'

– Mary-Kate Olsen

KEITH & MICK

These two cats have been at it for over 50 years – jamming, shredding, scrapping, getting up to mischief and making some of the best damn music the world has ever seen. As musical collaborators in the Rolling Stones, Mick Jagger and Keith Richards are one of the most successful partnerships in history, penning hits like 'Angie', 'Paint it Black', 'Gimme Shelter' and 'Sympathy for the Devil'. As friends, they're prone to discord and volatile bust-ups – but somehow they always get back together.

As bandmates, they've seen a lot together: from facing down the authorities who saw their rock 'n' roll ways as a threat to society, to literally standing trial together in 1967.

Sure, they've had their problems: Keith lost years to a drug haze; Mick took control of the band, and Keith resented him for it. At some points, the band has more or less broken up – but either love or money has always brought them back together.

And even when they claim to hate one another (sometimes very publicly, by way of tell-all memoirs), in the end, they've got one key thing on their side – and that's the music. Says Keith, 'With any band that has been around, even for a few years, not everybody likes everybody all the time. But maybe you have a need for that conversation to continue, and music is the one way you can do that. It's stronger than any of the other things that can get in the way.' And after half a century in each other's company, having created one of history's most important and influential rock bands, that's never gonna change.

'Sometimes I despise the man, others, I love that man so much. It's like your brother. I never had one, so he's my brother. That's the way it is, bless his heart.'

– Keith Richards

ALLEN & JACK

Sometimes two souls find each other like it's destiny – and when they collide, they change the whole world. So it was for Jack Kerouac and Allen Ginsberg: two passionate, intense visionaries whose friendship stretched from their wild university years, through decades of leading the counterculture charge, and ended only by Jack's all-too-early death.

Founding members of the Beat Generation, Jack and Allen found each other at Columbia University. Allen was the younger of the two – gawky, a bit naive, and ready to escape the boredom of middle-class America. Jack taught him about drinking, French Symbolist poetry and mysticism and together they became pioneers, experimenting enthusiastically with literature, drugs and sexuality. Their early days of friendship included being involved in a murder charge, catching obscenity charges and publishing some of the greatest writing that America had ever seen (Jack with *On the Road* and Allen with *Howl*).

They were also keen pen pals and wrote each other regularly for nearly 20 years, no matter what else was going on in their lives. An early letter from Jack to Allen shows just how passionate their friendship was: 'Please be reassured, angel, I think dearly of you whenever I do think of you, which is often, as I'm sure you do think of me often and dearly,' he wrote. While fame, travel and misadventure took them in different directions over the years, these two great minds of their generation remained the greatest of friends.

Jack predicted that their letters would go down in history: 'Someday, "The Letters of Allen Ginsberg to Jack Kerouac" will make America cry.'

MICHELLE & BUSY

Dawson's Creek **gave us so much – formative notions about falling in love, Dawson's cry face, a weakness for campy teen dramas** – but its most precious gift to us all is the friendship between Michelle Williams and Busy Phillips.

The two met through mutual friends just prior to Busy being cast on *Dawson's Creek* in 2001, and they eventually bonded via nights out together drinking cheap wine. Their time working together on the show sparked a love so pure and so long-lasting that we are truly not worthy to be in its presence.

Over the years, they've proven their love in so many ways (and cute Instagram snaps):

attending award shows together, taking obligatory bathroom selfies, holding hands on flights during take-off, showing up for each other's successes and being mad vocal about their BFF status (Busy once referred to Michelle as 'my heart' on Twitter and we still haven't recovered). Busy is godmother to Michelle's daughter, Matilda and Michelle even pierced Busy's ears for her while they were backstage at the Critics' Choice Awards – these are not things you could trust just anyone with.

The ultimate sign of their friendship? Not only have they been super supportive to one another and stood by each other through the best and worst times, but they also know how to take a selfie that captures both their best angles. And that is not nothing.

'I'm so in love with her. She's proof that the love of your life does not have to be a man! That's the love of my life right there.'

– Michelle Williams

FERRIS & CAMERON

Being a teenager sucks, and it sucks especially hard when you have to go to a dumb high school, surrounded by dumb teachers, and study things that have no relevance to your life. The only thing that can save you? Having a best friend to convince you to skip school and thus make your life worth living. Enter Ferris Bueller and Cameron Frye: two shining icons of friendship, truancy and breaking free from the bonds of boredom.

Ferris is charming, manipulative, irresponsible and completely narcissistic. He's the cool guy with a hot girlfriend, the guy everyone wants to be. Cameron is his opposite: alienated, a little bit emo, the poster child for teen angst. Together, they balance each other out: when he's with Ferris, Cameron is able to loosen up and get out of his comfort zone, ultimately leading him to confront his deep-seated passivity, anxiety and emotionally absent father; and being with Cameron inspires Ferris to think about someone other than himself for once ... for a minute, anyway. Like when Ferris literally steals a float in a street parade and gives an impromptu performance of 'Twist and Shout', just to give his bestie a thrill. 'It's one of my personal favourites and I want to dedicate it to a young man who doesn't think he's seen anything good today – Cameron Frye, this one's for you.'

Whether they're committing grand theft auto, contemplating art or faking an identity to gain access to a fancy restaurant, these two stick by each other (admittedly, for Cameron, it's sometimes under duress). But ultimately they're the kind of BFFs who'd do anything for one another – especially if it also means scoring a day off school.

'Ferris Bueller, you're my hero.'
– Cameron Frye

JAY & SILENT BOB

Can two small-time drug-dealers who spend all of their time hanging out in a convenience store parking lot and harassing passers-by be aspirational? When it comes to friendship goals, you bet they can. Jay and Silent Bob from Kevin Smith's View Askewniverse are best friends and literal partners in crime, who don't need nothing in life but each other's company (and maybe a blunt or two).

Sure, Jay is foulmouthed, obnoxious and has zero ambitions beyond getting high and partying, but he can't be faulted when it comes to his devotion to Silent Bob. And Silent Bob is equally steady in his love of Jay ... although you'll never hear him admit it. These two may be slackers, but they show up for each other. Whether they're fighting security guards, going up against renegade angels, or trying to stop an unauthorised biopic, they stick by each other through the good, the bad and the completely ridiculous.

There's so much in life that we don't have control over. But we do get to choose who we spend our days with – and you could do a lot worse than choosing a friend who just gets you. And if that means bonding over an appreciation of dick jokes and the need to avoid all of life's responsibilities, then so be it. Snootchie bootchies!

'I'm Jay, and this is my hetero life mate, Silent Bob.'

– Jay

EDDY & PATSY

Edina Monsoon and Patsy Stone of *Absolutely Fabulous* are two of a kind: boozy, badly behaved, self-indulgent, self-obsessed, utterly fabulous party girls who refuse to grow old gracefully ... or at all.

In a world that insists you have to play by the rules, Patsy and Eddy are an unapologetic breath of fresh air. They're mean. They're sassy. They smoke and drink and take drugs and don't give a damn what anyone thinks about it. And they look great. Do they party hard? Yes. Do they have any regrets? Also yes. But no matter how completely trashed they get, they'll always be there for one another (usually with a fresh bottle of vodka to take the edge off).

You could argue that they're not so much friends as they are the only two people who are able to stand each other's narcissism – but you'd be wrong. They're soulmates. Neither care about being socially acceptable. Both loathe being normal. Aside from shopping, their friendship is the most important thing in their lives. And the older they get, the more they need each other – who else is ever going to understand and accept them so completely?

As best friends, these two paragons of vice aren't just iconic, they're aspirational. They're a reminder to dress more fabulously, act more impulsively, and don't let boring people convince you to be boring. Sweetie, darling ... why be normal when you could be fun?

The show was based on a sketch written by lifelong comedy BFFs Dawn French and Jennifer Saunders. And actor Joanna Lumley credits her on-screen chemistry with Saunders to their real-life friendship.

FALKOR & BASTIAN

Best friends come in many forms – and sometimes that form might be a giant mythical creature that's part canine, part dragon and ready to show up to save you whenever you find yourself in a suboptimal situation. *The Neverending Story*'s Falkor is that friend: a resident of Fantasia, servant of the Childlike Empress, helper to the warrior Atreyu and best friend to Bastian Balthazar Bux.

About to die in the Swamps of Sadness? Falkor will be there. Need a to find a cure to save your Empress from being consumed by The Nothing? The luckdragon will come through. Need to get back at those bullies from your school for throwing you in the bin? Call on Falkor, my friend, and he will teach them a lesson they won't forget anytime soon.

But it's not just Falkor's blue fire-breathing abilities or willingness to use his powers to have Bastian's back that make him so great. He's also a fun guy to be around – kind of a cross between a wise old sage and a labrador. He always looks out for Bastian, and Bastian loves him like the best friend he is. And while we can't all travel to Fantasia (unless you happen to have a mysterious bookseller in your vicinity with just the right tome to take you there), if you can get yourself a buddy who looks at you the way Bastian looks at Falkor, you'll never have to be lonely again.

'Never give up and good luck will find you.'
– Falkor the luckdragon

DONNA & LAURA

There is nothing in the world that's stronger – or more complicated – than the friendship between teenage girls. Sometimes it's as intense as a love affair. Sometimes it's a brutal competition. Sometimes it feels like a death wish. For *Twin Peaks*' Laura Palmer and Donna Hayward, it was all of these things: loving, powerful, competitive, transformative, a way for both of them to escape the realities of their own lives.

Donna is trapped in her role as the good girl – she gets good grades, loves her parents, and looks after her little sisters. When she and Laura go out at night together, she borrows her best friend's clothes in the hope they'll make her mysterious and attractive to men too. She's always standing in Laura's shadow and she knows it. Laura is the girl with all the secrets, the homecoming queen who keeps cocaine in a locked box, who's been hurt so badly that all she can hope for is to be hurt on her own terms. Laura both envies Donna and pities her naivety. 'All my things have me in them,' she tells Donna. 'I don't want you to be like me.'

Together, they are like two halves of the same gold pendant – opposite but complementary, separate but joined, attuned to each other's edges in a way that suggests they're two halves of a whole. As friends, they remind us that sometimes our most profound connections are also our most complicated, and sometimes who we love is the biggest mystery of all.

'Donna, are you my best friend?'

– Laura Palmer

ROMY & MICHELE

No one has ever pulled off a high-school reunion with more panache than Romy White and Michele Weinberger. The bubbly, fashion-obsessed, totally fab Valley girls embody everything great about having a BFF who just gets you – they're always on the same wavelength and willing to play along with each other's silliest plans (say, having invented Post-It notes).

The duo are relatable in so many ways. At first they fret about how successful they are, the fact they don't have boyfriends, and what their high-school frenemies think about them. They try to change themselves to impress the people who made their lives miserable, and you know what? That doesn't make them happy either. Finally, they realise that the cool clique isn't all that, boyfriends aren't important and that the power of their friendship is the only thing that really matters. Case in point: when Michele's crush asks her to dance, she agrees on the condition that Romy can dance with them, resulting in the greatest three-way interpretive dance sequence ever to be set to Cyndi Lauper's 'Time After Time'.

If we can learn anything from Romy and Michele, it's that life after high school might not be exactly what you envisioned it to be and that success comes in many different forms. But as long as you've got your best friend at your side, there's really nothing that can stop you. Oh, and always dress exactly the way you want to – *especially* if it involves matchy-matchy sparkly minidresses.

'I think we should go back out there as ourselves, and just have fun like we always do. The hell with everyone else!'

– Michele Weinberger

As soon as I saw you ...

I knew an adventure was going to happen.

– Winnie the Pooh

BINGLEY & DARCY

When it comes to love, it's easy to be distracted by your crush's manners, wealth or how handsome he looks in his regimentals (why hello there, Mr Wickham). But if you really want to know what sort of man he is, take a look at how he treats his friends. If he seems like a proud, disagreeable sort, but he's a loyal and true friend, well ... perhaps he isn't all that bad.

Mr Bingley, from Jane Austen's classic *Pride and Prejudice*, is charming and gentlemanlike, with pleasant manners and a tendency to think the best of people. Conversely, his best mate, Mr Darcy, comes across as rude, bad-tempered, judgemental, and prone to offending wherever he goes (such a babe, though). Everyone thinks Darcy is a jerk, but not Bingley. Bingley sees through the prickly exterior to Darcy's good points – he's way ahead of Elizabeth Bennet on that one. And the love goes both ways. Perhaps in spite of himself, Darcy needs the unfailing optimism and sunny outlook that Bingley brings to his life, and he always tries to do right by his friend (and while he almost messed it all up by steering Bingley away from Jane, he only got involved because he cared so much).

It may be a truth universally acknowledged that a single man in possession of a good fortune must be in want of a wife, but it's equally true that a man needs a good bromance, too. And you would be hard-pressed to find a better match than Fitzwilliam Darcy and Charles Bingley.

'Mr Darcy is uncommonly kind to Mr Bingley, and takes a prodigious deal of care of him.'

– Elizabeth Bennet

THELMA & LOUISE

***Thelma and Louise* is an iconic film about two badass Texas broads who take off for the road trip of a lifetime and discover that all they need in this life is each other.** Thelma Dickinson and Louise Sawyer are the kind of friends who take a gamble on freedom and risk everything to be together.

When we first meet Thelma, she's married to a deadbeat dude who demands she seek his permission before heading out on a fishing trip with her best friend, Louise. But when the two of them stop for a drink, things go completely pear-shaped: a jerk at the bar tries to rape Thelma in the parking lot, so Louise shuts it down with the help of a .38 calibre Colt.

On the run, the duo travel across America in an epic road trip that involves holding up a store at gunpoint, blowing up a truck, and getting it on with a very young and stupidly handsome Brad Pitt.

Thelma and Louise are each other's protectors and liberators. Together, they're empowered to express and assert themselves – awakening a sense purpose that life had crushed out of them. Thelma says, 'Everything looks different now. You feel like that, too, like you got something to look forward to?'

When the police finally catch up with them, Thelma and Louise refuse to say goodbye to their newfound freedom and, instead of surrendering, they make the ultimate choice as besties: to make a run for it. 'Let's not get caught,' says Thelma. 'Let's keep going.' When it comes to film friendships, the movie's indelible final images, of Thelma and Louise firmly clasping their hands together in solidarity before gunning their T-Bird into the Grand Canyon, are about as iconic as it gets.

> ***'Louise ... no matter what happens, I'm glad I came with you.'***
>
> *– Thelma Dickinson*

SETH & JAMES

There are few Hollywood friendships as weirdly compelling as that of Seth Rogen and James Franco. Best friends since they met on the set of the excellent and tragically short-lived series *Freaks and Geeks*, much of their charm can be found in the fact that they are so unashamedly into one another.

No matter where their careers take them, they always come back to each other. They write movies to star in together. They hang out in their downtime. On one occasion, they jumped out of a cake together. Seth threw James a bar mitzvah (even though he was technically a little old for it), and James once wrote a series of poems about the power of their friendship. Heck, they even made out passionately on a motorcycle in their Kim and Kanye video parody (or should that be tribute?) 'Bound 3'.

As creative partners, they bring out each other's best (if your BFF doesn't encourage you to embrace your weirdest ideas, they're really not on the level). As buddies, they enthusiastically embrace the bromance. They love each other for what is on the inside. They're always down to nude up in each other's company. They accept each other's unique desires and fantasies (if James wants to paint erotic portraits of his friend, that's totally fine).

And if your friendship remains intact after you've been blamed for almost unwittingly starting a war with North Korea, you know there's nothing that can tear you apart.

'If anybody should paint Seth naked, it should be me.'

– James Franco

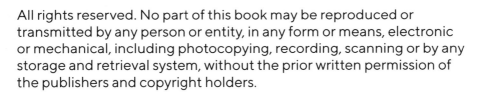

Smith Street Books

Published in 2018 by Smith Street Books
Melbourne | Australia
smithstreetbooks.com

ISBN: 978-1-925418-68-2

All rights reserved. No part of this book may be reproduced or transmitted by any person or entity, in any form or means, electronic or mechanical, including photocopying, recording, scanning or by any storage and retrieval system, without the prior written permission of the publishers and copyright holders.

Copyright text © Nadia Bailey
Copyright design © Smith Street Books
Copyright illustrations © Juppi Juppsen

CIP data is available from the National Library of Australia

Publisher: Hannah Koelmeyer
Designer: Susan Hardjono
Illustrator: Juppi Juppsen

Printed & bound in China by C&C Offset Printing Co., Ltd.
Book 48

10 9 8 7 6 5 4 3 2 1

302
.34
BAI

Bailey, N.
The world's best BFFs.
Aurora P.L. MAY18
33164300333338